Jasmine's Journey

A Story of Overcoming Obstacles
By Jasmine Simmons
Mom Insights By Tisha Simmons

AuthorHouse™
1663 Liberty Drive
Bloomington, IN 47403
www.authorhouse.com
Phone: 833-262-8899

Because of the dynamic nature of the Internet, any web addresses or links contained in this book may have changed since publication and may no longer be valid. The views expressed in this work are solely those of the author and do not necessarily reflect the views of the publisher, and the publisher hereby disclaims any responsibility for them.

Any people depicted in stock imagery provided by Getty Images are models, and such images are being used for illustrative purposes only.

Certain stock imagery © Getty Images.

This book is printed on acid-free paper.

ISBN: 978-1-6655-4967-7 (sc)
ISBN: 979-8-8230-0738-2 (hc)
ISBN: 978-1-6655-5067-3 (e)

Library of Congress Control Number: 2022900946

Print information available on the last page.

Published by AuthorHouse 06/30/2023

authorHOUSE®

Jasmine's Journey
A Story of Overcoming Obstacles

by Jasmine Simmons

Mom Insights by Tisha Simmons

Dedication

This book is dedicated to children and adults that have vascular anomalies or other rare medical issues that impact their daily lives. We know your struggles. We hope this book will encourage you to continue your journey!

Silhouette images are used in this book to allow the reader to be a part of Jasmine's journeys. Everywhere you see a silhouette, imagine yourself there with Jasmine.

The purple hearts represent the presence of the vascular anomalies throughout Jasmine's adventures. Although the anomalies are there, her journey never ends and is not hindered!

A Message from Jasmine:

Find the miracles in your moment, no matter how difficult your moment may be!

I'm Jasmine and I love riding my bike. I mean, I **REALLY** love riding my bike. If I could, I would ride my bike *all* day and *all* night.

When I am home, I ride my bike up and down our driveway. As I ride, I listen to the crunch of the rocks under my tires. I grip the handlebars tight and *zoom* down the hill. My puppy chases behind me trying to keep up.

I ride my bike through our bike trails and through the woods. I love the feel of the cool wind on my face as I ride over the bumpy ground. The squirrels scurry up the trees trying to get a better view of me riding my bike while the birds watch from above. I am free and nothing bothers me while I ride my bike!

My bike takes me on long, peaceful rides. My bike takes me on fast, short trips. I love my bike and my bike loves me.

My bike and my imagination help me ride past my problems and worries. They help me get over being in the hospital, going to doctors' appointments, having procedures, and not feeling well. My imagination helps me deal with the very serious medical issues that I have.

I am like thousands of other kids that have vascular anomalies. A vascular anomaly happens when some of your veins grow differently. They are sometimes called malformations. They can hurt really bad. I have a vascular malformation on my back. I once had nine of them grow in my intestines. I was really sick and it took a long time for me to get better.

Not feeling well can be hard and sometimes I get sad. That's when I remember all of the wonderful things that I have to be thankful for. I have a family that loves me, friends that send me cards, and teachers that care. I also have doctors that are working extra hard to help me feel better. And I have my bike and my imagination to help me escape when I need to.

Sometimes during procedures, I imagine myself riding my bike on the beach beside the water. I can smell the salty water as I ride by. I can hear the waves crashing against the sand. I see the dolphins in the distance. It is so peaceful there.

Sometimes when the nurse takes my blood, I imagine riding my bike to the moon. I pretend that the needle stick is me taking off into space. I hold my breath as my bike becomes my rocket. 5... 4... 3... 2... 1...*Blast off!*
Whew! It's over! Now I can return to Earth!

When I am in the hospital, I like to imagine riding my bike on new adventures. My bike and my imagination are always there ready to take me away from my problems and my fears. I can depend on my bike to help me through the tough times.

BRIGHTER DAYS ARE COMING!

I have learned that no matter how hard things get for me, there is always someone that is having a harder time. Like Joey, he has not been able to eat solid food for more than a year. Olivia has chemo treatments and feels really tired all of the time. And Joy, she has been in the hospital for months and has had two surgeries. She seems really sad sometimes because she misses her friends at school.

Remembering how brave these kids are helps me to get over my bad days. Instead of crying, I imagine riding my bike on silly adventures. Instead of being angry, I pretend to be somewhere else. That's when things don't seem so bad and I know I can make it through.

I'M ONLY A BIKE RIDE AWAY!

I have learned to be brave when times get tough. When I want to give up, I think of all the good things that I have in my life. I also imagine being on adventures and feeling my very best.

I know that things may seem hard right now, but remember *this will not last forever.* If you need to escape on an adventure, imagine joining me on the beach or on the moon. Maybe you can join me on an exciting ride down the mountains. Together, we can get through this. *I'm only a bike ride away!*

MOM INSIGHTS

SUPPORTING THE EMOTIONAL NEEDS OF A LOVED ONE

Parent Notes:

My daughter Jasmine was born with vascular anomalies. At birth, she had a very visible malformation on her back that required years of visits to specialists, treatments, and hospital stays. At the age of seven, she began having dramatic drops in her hemoglobin. After a year of blood transfusions and iron infusions, the cause of the dangerous changes in her hemoglobin were still unknown. For anyone that has heard "we don't know the cause" from a physician, you understand exactly how difficult the unknown can be.

During a three week stay in the hospital, a vascular malformation was found in her small intestines. After a major surgery, we were sure she would be alright and on the road to a great recovery. However, several weeks later, she was back in the hospital undergoing a seven-hour surgery. This time, eight malformations were removed from her small intestines. The surgery was followed by a slow and painful recovery. The experience left our family with both physical and emotional scares that are still healing to this day.

It wasn't until after our most difficult times in the hospital were over that we were able to evaluate the emotional, spiritual, and physical toll that this medical trauma had taken on our family. There wasn't a guide. There wasn't a "what to do now" plan of action. We were left with all of these feelings. Feelings of grief, fear, sadness, pain, happiness, thankfulness, and relief. We were left with just our feelings. Each of the feelings had equal value and each feeling impacted not only our emotional health, but our physical health as well.

As a result of our trauma, Jasmine and I decided to provide a "how to guide" for the next family and the next child, so that you know that all of your feelings are valid. All of your feelings have an important place in your family's journey and you will get through this!

Earlier, Jasmine shared how she faces the challenges of undergoing procedures, surgeries, blood draws, and other challenges by remembering how much she enjoys riding her bike. Over the next few pages, I will share how I provide the support that Jasmine needs in order to continue her medical journey.

I am not an expert on coping with medical traumas. I am not a licensed therapist. I am a mom with experience and I want to provide others with the tools that have helped me navigate some of our family's most challenging life experiences. I have included reflections and mistakes that I have made during this journey to help others avoid making the same mistakes. I hope that my "Mom Insights" provide others with the "how to guide" that so many go without when dealing with traumatic medical events.

Mom Insights: Supporting the Emotional Needs of a Loved One
Written by an Experienced Mom: Tisha Simmons

Insight #1: Be Proactive, Assertive, and Respectful

We are our children's biggest advocates. We know them better than anyone else. Therefore, if you know something is wrong, advocate for your child. It is important to remember that physicians are human. They don't know everything, but they care enough to hear your concerns. It is important to have a team of caregivers for your child and have open lines of communications with them.

Be an active part of the medical process that your child is going through. Keep a journal of things that you notice at home and things your child's teachers tell you. All of this information is valuable when trying to determining what is going on medically with your child.

Reflections:

I often think back when Jasmine was seven and starting second-grade at a new school. She began struggling and had trouble remembering skills that she learned in previous grades. I talked to her teacher, the principal, and took her to the pediatrician numerous times. Everyone believed her struggles were the result of her adjusting to a new school. However, I knew there was more going on. I watched a child that once recited bible verses from memory, solved math problems in her head, and read a grade level ahead, forget how to add and subtract. I felt so helpless. Nothing explained what was happening to my child. I continued to take her to the pediatrician and I continued to express my concerns.

After struggling for months, Jasmine was referred to a neurologist where she was examined thoroughly. Her hemoglobin was checked later that day for the first time. Before that day, none of the physicians she had seen ever suspected that Jasmine was anemic with a dangerously low hemoglobin level. That same day, she was admitted into the children's hospital where she spent several days. She received both blood transfusions and iron infusions.

My persistence got her the treatment that she desperately needed. She began feeling better and the following school year she was back on grade level. It took another year to determine that bleeding from vascular anomalies in her intestines were the cause of the drops in her hemoglobin.

I share this story to demonstrate the importance of knowing your child and being proactive about the healthcare your child receives. Significant changes in behavior, a decline in performance in school, and/or a decrease in participation in social activities are all warning signs that something is wrong. Do not ignore those red flags. Be proactive and assertive, in a respectful manner, when it comes to your child's health. You are your child's biggest advocate. Even the best physicians can overlook things that you as a parent notice.

Insight #2: Be Age-Appropriately Honest with Your Child

As I stated before, Jasmine was born with a visible vascular malformation on her spine. My husband and I made a conscious effort to explain her medical issues to her in terms that she understood. We showed her x-rays and MRI images of the malformation. We talked to her about how the treatments were helping her and why we had to travel so far to the hospital. We never told her that procedures "wouldn't hurt" or "you won't remember a thing". Instead, we made it a point to tell her that everything that she was going through was temporary and that we would always be there to support her. Reassuring her allowed her to find comfort in knowing that she would be able to move past the pain and trauma after each procedure.

Reflections:

During Jasmine's hospital stays, we would often visit the playrooms. We met kids that had unimaginable health issues. Because the kids had tubes attached to their stomachs, oxygen tubes in their noses, and were frail from surgeries, I thought those kids were suffering. It wasn't until I began to see how those children interacted with others that I learned how resilient kids are. They can truly "take a lick'in and keep on tick'in". What stood out the most to me was how informed most of the kids were about their health issues. They were able to vocalize their challenges and discuss their medical issues with others. Hearing Jasmine share her experiences with others helped me realize that my husband and I had made the right decision by not hiding things from her. Having an understanding of what she had already overcome, gave her hope that she was strong enough to continue the fight. From this, I learned the importance of children understanding their own physical challenges. It's true; you don't know what you can overcome until you have overcome it.

I know that some truths are harder to face than others. I have cried many times because of the truths that I have had to tell my child. However, it is easier for her to face the challenges that she knows about than to be left alone with the mysteries of the unknown.

Insight #3: Stay Positive in Front of Your Child

This may seem simple, but often as parents it easy to allow our emotions to control our actions. A disparaging comment about a nurse, a doctor, or even a social worker, can cause your child to have unnecessary anxiety about the care that he or she is receiving. It is in your child's best interest to believe that the care that is received is the best that's available. Any crack in that foundation can cause your child to lose trust in the medical treatment that is needed. Be mindful of the comments you make while in the presence of your child. I learned this lesson the hard way.

Reflections:

After another day of bad news at the hematologist's office, I found myself in the parking garage crying and having a complete mental meltdown. I was convinced that the nurse practitioner could have cared less about my child's needs and I worried that no one would ever figure out why Jasmine was having issues with her hemoglobin. The weight of being told to bring her back for a blood transfusion the next day instead of getting her help that day was too much for me to handle. So, I sat in the car and cried. I mean, I really cried. Soon I had a crying child sitting beside me repeating how much the nurse did not care about her. I remember hearing the negative words seeping from her trembling lips. "My God. What have I done?", I thought to myself. I needed Jasmine to have confidence in those that were treating her. I needed her to know that everyone involved was working hard on her behalf. However, at that moment, I did not consider the fact that she was listening to me. She was soaking in all my emotions as I complained about her care. She was doubting that she was getting the care she needed to get better. I created a crack in her foundation.

After finally finding the strength to crank up the car and leave, I received a phone call from the hematologist's office. I was instructed to take Jasmine to the hospital where she would receive several blood transfusions that day. While I was crying and having a complete meltdown, I was unaware that the practitioner was working on getting her a room in the children's hospital. My feelings about her were wrong and they caused Jasmine to have the same wrong feelings. My negative feelings caused Jasmine to believe that someone on her care team was not giving 100 percent towards her care and that was wrong.

This story is one that I do not want you to have. After that day, I was intentional about praising the doctors and nurses that treated Jasmine. I spoke nothing but praises about the child life coaches that came in. I smiled at the volunteers that brought in dogs for her to pet. I wanted her to believe that she had the BEST care in the world and everyone was working to get her better. That was what Jasmine needed and as her parent that was what I had to give.

You will have days that you feel like your child is not receiving the best care. However, remember, it is not in any physician's interest to provide patients with subpair care. If there are misunderstandings about your child's care, make it a point to discuss your concerns with the doctor without your child being present. Remember, each hospital has a chain of command for providers. Use your resources if needed, but always keep things positive in the presence of your child.

Insight #4: Communicate with Family and Friends as You See Fit

As humans we want to be there for one another. This is especially true when a child is sick or has medical issues. Loved ones want to connect and communicate with you to make sure that everything is okay. However, when your child is in the hospital, you often don't have the time to communicate with others and that is okay! I struggled with finding a balance in communicating with others the last time Jasmine had a very long stay in the hospital.

Reflections:

I often felt "some type of way" when I received phone calls or text from people saying "why didn't you tell me Jasmine was in the hospital" or "you should have called me". Often when I read those messages, I felt a sense of anger. I wanted to yell "I didn't call because I haven't slept for more than 3 hours over the last 3 days", "I didn't call because my child needed me to help her get out of the bed", or "I didn't call because I simply didn't have the energy to talk". The truth is, I didn't call because I was emotionally drained and sharing my emotions would have left me completely bankrupt with nothing left to give to Jasmine. I could not stop and think or share my feelings because then I would have to acknowledge my own fears, hurt, sorrow, grief, pain, and worry. Yes, I would have had to acknowledge that I was barely hanging on by a thread and one moment alone to think about my feelings would have caused me to have an emotional breakdown. Those people had the best intentions, but simply didn't understand the stress I was under.

After months of extended stays in the hospital, Jasmine's health finally improved and she was able to return to some of her normal routines. It was at that point that I realized that I had done what I needed to do to get my family through the trauma of dealing with some very serious medical issues. To get us through those times, I did not return phone calls or texts. I did not update people. I did not ask for help. That is what got me through the trauma. However, I unintentionally hurt the feelings of many people that I value. I left people out of my circle that would have prayed for us, provided us homecooked meals, or even ran errands for us.

I want others to learn from my mistakes in this area. It is okay to limit your communications with others. However, there is a way to limit your communications and still allow others an opportunity to help you through the process.

Here's how:

    A. Have one or two trusted individuals that act as your messengers. Update those individuals with a simple text. Allow them to be your voice to the world, while you handle things with your child.

    B. Don't feel guilty if you don't return a few calls or if you don't respond to a text. Your focus should always be on your child's well-being. People will understand, and if they don't, they should not be in your circle anyway.

    C. It is okay if you chose not to share what you and your family are going through. Although this is a hard decision to make, sometimes it is easier to share your problems after you have overcome the challenges the problems created. As long as you are making the decision not to share based on what your child needs, it's probably the right decision. If sharing with certain people adds additional stress to your lives, then don't share. Most importantly, don't feel guilty for not sharing.

My Final Insight: Find the Miracles in Your Moment

I know that this is hard. I know it's hard to "look at the bright side". I get it. I've been there. I have felt completely helpless, hopeless, and heartbroken. However, when I focus on the miracles in each moment, I see that there is always something to be thankful for. Each time that Jasmine is in the hospital, each procedure that she has, and after each tear I see her cry, I remember that she's going home with me. I get to hold her again. I get to hear her voice, and I get to listen to her breath. Over our journey, I have met mothers that weren't as blessed.

Reflections:

One late afternoon after a doctor's visit, Jasmine was sent to the emergency room again. It was busy, but nothing seemed out of the ordinary. After being checked in, we waited in the small room for what seemed like hours. Our visits to the emergency room had never taken this long. As my concern started to grow, I began hearing loud screams and yells. Pleads of "don't leave me son" and "fight, fight" rang through the building. The sorrow felt in that mother's voice pierced my soul and I began to pray for her. I was not sure what had happened, but I knew their situation was far more serious than ours at the moment.

As the seriousness of the situation grew, time seemed to stop. Then the words "No God, Nooo" echoed throughout the building. Unimaginable pain filled every inch of the emergency center. The mother's screams turned to heartbreaking shrieks of pain. My heart would not let me open the door of our room. I did not want to see the face of the mother who had just lost one of her most precious gifts. As I prayed for that mother, I held my own child tight knowing that I would be able to take her home with me; if not that day, one day. That mother did not have that option.

I remember that mother's pain often. I never met her, but I cry for her often. I pray that she is restored and at peace. In that moment, her pain gave me purpose. I thank God that I now see the miracles in the moments no matter how hard the moments may be.

Over the years, Jasmine's medical journeys have created a new outlook on life for me. I know that no matter what I'm going through, someone else is facing a more difficult situation. I remind Jasmine of this as she manages the daily challenges that having vascular anomalies bring. In every situation, there is something to be thankful for. I encourage others to take the time to find the miracles in your moment, no matter how difficult your moment may be!

Note from the Authors

Thank you for taking the time to read about our journey. We hope that through our words both you and your child will find the strength to push through to another day. We would love for you to share your stories of overcoming challenges on Jasmine's website: www.jasminethekidauthor.com

As you know, medical expenses for ongoing treatments are expensive. Please consider donating to your local children's hospital. Your donations will help support families in need.

FIND THE MIRACLES
IN YOUR MOMENT,
NO MATTER HOW DIFFICULT
YOUR MOMENT MAY BE!

Printed in the United States
by Baker & Taylor Publisher Services